Practical Punctuation

Practical Punctuation

Ian Gordon

Principal Lecturer in English, College of St Mark and St John, Plymouth

HEINEMANN
EDUCATIONAL

Heinemann Educational Publishers
Halley Court, Jordan Hill, Oxford OX2 8EJ
a division of Reed Educational & Professional Publishing Ltd

MELBOURNE AUCKLAND
FLORENCE PRAGUE MADRID ATHENS
SINGAPORE TOKYO SAO PAULO
CHICAGO PORTSMOUTH (NH) MEXICO
IBADAN GABORONE JOHANNESBURG
KAMPALA NAIROBI

ISBN 0 435 10266 4

97 98 16 15 14 13 12 11

Printed in Great Britain by
Athenæum Press Ltd, Gateshead, Tyne & Wear

Contents

5 DASHES

6 COLONS

7 SEMI-COLONS

8 BRACKETS

9 QUOTATION MARKS, ITALICS, UNDERLINING

10 DIRECT SPEECH

11 PUNCTUATING LETTERS

12 REVISION

Introduction

Good punctuation is essential for writing to be easily and rapidly understood.

Unfortunately, it is much easier to check spelling than punctuation. A quick look into a dictionary tells us clearly and surely how a word may be spelled; but there are no dictionaries for punctuation. Sentences cannot be arranged in alphabetical order for reference. Each sentence is a fresh pattern of words, and provides a fresh challenge. Moreover, for punctuation there are generally not so much rules, as guidelines.

Still, there *are* some firm rules, and a great number of guidelines, and these can be listed and quite easily learnt or referred to. This small book provides such a list, and it is intended to serve two purposes.

1) It should provide a sound, well-organized, and interesting course in punctuation.
2) Equally, it should form a convenient reference book, a desk companion as close to a 'punctuation dictionary' as possible, which can be easily consulted whenever in doubt about some point of punctuation.

As a course book, it can be used by students in Britain, and just as well by those overseas. It can be used at any stage, but it is specially recommended for students preparing for public examinations, and for those who feel they need to 'brush up' their punctuation for study purposes or work. With class use in mind, sentences for illustration and exercises have been made as varied as possible in subject matter and construction, and it is possible a teacher may find some of the sentences useful stimuli for composition work — starting off stories, and so on. On the other hand, a private pupil, because of the guidance given (as in the revision quiz, Exercise 31, page 59) and the strong control of the exercises, should be able to complete the course on his own without any difficulty. These exercises have been so devised that the exercises following a section test either only that particular section, or only the sections dealt with up to that point in the book. All punctuation marks not yet discussed are provided. In this way, the testing is controlled, guided, and systematic.

For reference purposes, all rules and guidelines have been clearly tabulated and numbered. Teachers using the book with a class may find it convenient to use at any rate some of these numbers when marking the more common punctuation errors in students' compositions. Thus 57 ringed in the margin would indicate that the name of a book or film has not been marked off — and the student must find the error and correct it himself, using this handbook.

Even if you are *not* working through this book as a course, and intend to use it only for reference purposes, you are still strongly advised to read through the whole book first — it is after all short — even though you do not complete the exercises, to get a 'feel' of the contents and layout.

Finally, remember that punctuation is in many ways an art. This book provides mainly leading principles of that art. Close observation of printed texts and constant reference to this book should help you acquire both a knowledge of these leading principles and also an appreciation of how useful a tool punctuation is in helping you to achieve your main aims in writing — to be immediately and unambiguously understood, and to be read with pleasure.

1   Capitals and Hyphens

Capitals

Note: 'initial capital' means a capital letter used as the first letter of a word.

1 Beginning of sentences

An initial capital is used for the first word of a sentence.

Examples: My brother is six years old. He likes animals. Yesterday he went to a zoo for the first time.

2 Proper nouns

Initial capitals are used for proper nouns — such as the names of:

a person —
  Judith
  Pierre

a country —
  India
  China

a street —
  High Street
  Fifth Avenue

a geographical feature —
  Mount Everest
  the Suez Canal

an institution —
  the Stock Exchange
  the Bank of England

a business company —
  Heinemann Educational Books
  British Oxygen Company

a day of the week —
  Tuesday
  Friday

a month —
  April
  November

a town or city —
  Liverpool
  New York

a language —
  Spanish
  Urdu

a political party —
  the Labour Party
  the Liberal Party

a historical period —
  the Renaissance
  the French Revolution

a race —   a festival —
   Europeans   Christmas
   Asians   Ramadan

an organization —
   the International Red Cross
   the United Nations

3 The Deity

Initial capitals are used for names of the Deity.

Examples: God, the Almighty, Allah, the Holy Spirit

Capitals are also often used for pronouns referring to God.

Examples: He, Him, You, Thee, Thou, Who, Whose

When referring to pagan gods, write god/gods (no capital), but use a capital for their names.

Examples: Mars, god of war, was the son of the goddess Juno.

4 Adjectives from proper nouns

As a general rule, adjectives from proper nouns begin with a capital letter.

Examples: Chinese, Indian, Parisian, Roman

But there are some exceptions for the names of common objects.

Examples: french windows, morocco leather, asian flu, diesel engine, arabic numerals

5 Family relationships — such as father, mother, uncle, aunt, etc.

a) Use an initial capital for relationship word alone.

   Examples: I hope Uncle will not be too late, because Grandmother is rather tired, and so is Father.

   note: *brother, sister* and *cousin* are not used in this way.

b) Use initial capitals for relationship word plus a proper name.

   Examples: I asked Aunt Alice, and Uncle Joe, and Cousin Louise to come and stay with us.

   note: *brother* and *sister* are not used in this way.

c) Use initial capitals for the relationship word plus proper name if a possessive adjective precedes it, *except for brother and sister.*

Examples: Has my Uncle George got the tickets yet?
I do not know his sister Jane well.

d) Do not use an initial capital if there is no proper name, and an article or possessive adjective precedes the relationship word.

Examples: We asked our uncle to give up work.
The aunt in Canada is a nurse.
My sister is not home yet.
She gave her mother a present.

e) Initial capitals are always used for relationship words when applied to priests or members of religious orders.

Examples: Father Brown (a priest), Brother Joseph (a monk), Sister Teresa (a nun), Mother Superior (head of a religious house)

6 Books, plays, films, newspapers, musical works

Use initial capitals for the first word, and all following main words in the titles of books, plays, etc. (Do *not* use initial capitals for articles, conjunctions, or prepositions when they are not the first word.)

Examples: *A Look at Indian Architecture, She Stoops to Conquer, Six Years in a Leper Colony, The Daily Telegraph, New World Symphony*

7 Personal titles

a) Always use initial capitals for a personal title *plus* a proper name.

Examples: Queen Elizabeth, King George, President Kennedy, Sir James Morris, Lord Dennery, Nurse Thompson, Sergeant Ahmed

b) Use an initial capital for a personal title without a proper name when:

(i) the personal title is used to address someone in direct speech;

Example: 'Well, Doctor, is my father better?'

(ii) referring to a particular person holding a particular job.

Examples: The Secretary read the letter while the Chairman sat silent.
The Prime Minister broadcast to the nation.

But do not use capitals when speaking of a job in a general way.

Examples: My sister is a secretary.
I want to become an engineer.

8 Verse

Use an initial capital letter for the first word in each line of verse.

Example: Two men look out through the same bars;
One sees mud — and one sees stars.

note: Letters and Direct Speech
See page 57 for the special use of capitals in letters.
See page 49 for the special use of capitals in direct speech.

WARNING — CAPITALS: Do *not* use capitals for:
a) the seasons — spring, summer, autumn, winter
b) compass points — north, south, east, west, unless part of the name of a region — e.g. the West (for the western part of the USA); the East (for the Orient); Northern Ireland; the Western Hemisphere   .
However, capitals are used for the abbreviations of compass points: NE (north-east), SW (south-west), etc.
c) school subjects — history, biology, physics, chemistry (but languages need a capital — English, Arabic, Japanese, etc.)

Exercise 1

Put capitals where needed in the following sentences.
1 i asked my brother paul if he had read *a year in the amazon basin.*
2 we study french and english, but not german at our school.
3 an irish nun, sister mary, teaches physics and chemistry at st mary's school.

4 in history we are now reading about the second world war with miss black.

5 my uncle bill has just bought a new rolls-royce silver cloud motorcar, but he won't give me his old ford.

6 when superintendent walker shouted at him, the policeman at the door let us in.

7 the eiffel tower attracts many thousands of overseas visitors, many of them american, especially in spring, when paris is at its best.

8 i should like to own a leica, perhaps the most famous of west german cameras.

9 i think that mother will take a short holiday in august or late july.

10 she will probably go with my elder sister rose to singapore or malaysia.

11 i bought *the times* from smith's in regent street, and read that the thames was in flood near my home in oxford.

12 when we were in amsterdam last summer we saw rembrandt's *the night watch* in the rijksmuseum.

13 one of the nurses took me to see matron, who explained that doctor snelling had seen gillian, and said she had pneumonia.

14 the newspapers here are full of stories about the miss world competition.

15 i think myself miss argentina will win the competition.

16 even the most faithful christians sometimes wonder why god in his wisdom allows so much suffering in the world.

17 the queen and the president of france stopped to be photographed before they left by car for buckingham palace.

18 according to homer, and all other greek poets, ares, the god of war, was the son of zeus and hera.

19 a new science laboratory was opened just after christmas by sir brian jackson, the distinguished scientist and author of *a history of scientific thought*.

20 i think uncle charles brought back a valuable collection of china from the east as well as some persian rugs.

Hyphens

Hyphens are used:
either a) to divide a single word because there is not room for the whole of that word in the line
or b) to join two separate words into a compound word
or c) to combine a word with a prefix or suffix.

9 Dividing words

Be careful to:

a) divide a word by syllables, without separating letters which belong closely to each other

> ***Examples:*** During the summer, we occasion-
> ally went to the park.
> *not:* During the summer we occasi-
> onally went to the park.
>
> My grandfather is find-
> ing it difficult to get about.
> *not:* My grandfather is fin-
> ding it difficult to get about.

b) write the hyphen at the end of the line, not at the beginning of the next line.

10 Compound words

There are few sure rules to the use of hyphens in compound words. Observation and a good dictionary are the best guides, but the following points are useful.

a) Use a hyphen if the second part of a compound word begins with a capital letter.

> ***Examples:*** anti-Communist, Anglo-Chinese, pro-British

b) Use a hyphen to form compound numbers when a multiple of ten is joined to a unit.

> ***Examples:*** twenty-one, thirty-three, forty-nine

But hyphens are *not* used with other parts of higher compound numbers.

> ***Examples:*** six thousand, four hundred and twenty-seven;
> twenty-eight thousand, four hundred and eighty-one

c) Use a hyphen when a number is combined with an adjective.

> ***Examples:*** The party of soldiers was sixty-strong.
> There were thirty-odd people in the room. (Compare the
> totally different meaning of: There were thirty odd people
> in the room.)

d) Use a hyphen when a number is combined with a noun of extent of time or space etc. to form an adjective.

Examples: a five-year sentence,   a three-foot rule,
a two-year contract,   a twenty-year lease,
twentieth-century literature,   a fifth-form pupil

WARNING — HYPHENS: No hyphen should be used in such constructions as: a sentence of five years, literature of the twentieth century.

11 Prefixes and suffixes

As a rule, prefixes and suffixes are *not* separated from the stem word.

Examples: overtake   unfasten   armful   clockwise

But hyphens are generally used:
a) to separate two identical adjacent letters, usually vowels, but sometimes consonants

Examples: ski-ing   pre-eminent   co-operate
re-entry   glow-worm

b) to distinguish words which have a different meaning with and without the hyphen

Examples: re-form and reform
re-bound and rebound

c) after *non*

Examples: non-combatant   non-starter

d) after *co*

Examples: co-education   co-pilot   (but coefficient)

e) before *like*

Examples: sheep-like   ant-like   (but *like* is part of many common words: childlike, warlike)

f) after *self*

Examples: self-interest   self-important

12 Dates and routes

The hyphen can often have the meaning of *to* in adjectival phrases.

Examples: the 1914-18 war, the New York-Lisbon air route, the Hong Kong-Kowloon ferry

WARNING: Never write 'from 1914-18' — write 'from 1914 to 1918' or 'between 1914 and 1918'

13 Phrases and clauses used as adjectives

Examples: It was a run-of-the-mill job.
He had a take-it-or-leave-it attitude.

WARNING: Write 'I told him he could take it or leave it'.

14 To indicate stammering

Example: 'G-g-give me th-th-that b-b-book,' he stammered.

Exercise 2

Put capitals and hyphens as needed in the following sentences.

1 my father served in the 1939 45 war.
2 she had an i'm better that you and you know it look about her.
3 my cousin sylvia is very self centred. she refuses to help aunt louise at all.
4 many things we take for granted today, such as inter continental air travel, would have been considered far fetched ideas only half a century ago.
5 there are twenty one young people in my son's class at the anglo spanish institute.

2 Full Stops, Question Marks, Exclamation Marks

Full Stops

15 Complete sentences

Full stops mark off complete sentences — groups of words containing at least one main verb, and making complete sense by themselves.

Examples: I **like** chess.
When it is dark, we **shall light** a fire.
My sister **hopped, skipped,** and **jumped** with delight.
After a long and tiring search, we **found** some size 9 shoes at a large store in town.

(The main verbs are in bold type.)

16 Incomplete sentences

In some modern writing, full stops are placed after groups of words which would not traditionally be called complete sentences, that is, after groups of words not containing a main verb. This is often done to convey excitement and suspense.

Example: He must get away. At once. To Greece. To India. The Pacific. Anywhere.

WARNING: Remember that using full stops in this way is effective because it is unusual. As a general rule use full stops only after complete sentences.

17 Abbreviations and contractions

You can either use a full stop or not for:
a) abbreviations ending with the same letter as the full word

Examples: Dr. or Dr for 'Doctor'
Rd. or Rd for 'Road'

b) abbreviations of countries and organizations.

Examples: U.S.A. or USA for United States of America
B.B.C. or BBC for British Broadcasting Corporation

Use a full stop after an abbreviation (other than countries and organizations) not ending with the same letter as the full word.

Examples: Co. for 'Company'
etc. for Latin *et cetera*, 'and the rest'
e.g. for Latin *exempli gratia*, 'for example'
i.e. for Latin *id est*, 'that is'

WARNING: Never place two full stops together. If a sentence ends with an abbreviated word, only one full stop should be used.

Example: My brother works for A.C. Black and Co.

18 The decimal point

Examples: a .303 rifle   £25.75   67.98 metres

19 Incomplete quotations

A series of full stops is used to indicate either an incomplete quotation, or a break in speech. The break may be at the beginning or end, or in the middle.

Examples: ' ". . . or to take up arms against a sea of troubles." How does that quotation begin?'
' "A little learning is a dangerous thing . . ." I can never remember the next line.'
'And if you go to the police with your story . . .' The stranger smiled and spoke softly, but he looked dangerous.
The report said, 'All shops . . . should stay open . . . until six o'clock.'

Exercise 3

Put capitals, hyphens, and full stops as needed in the following sentences. *Do not use any commas.*

Each of the following examples consists of *two* sentences:

1 mrs bryant is away she'll be back in a week's time
2 i should like to go to hong kong one day my pen friend lives there

3 i do not like travelling by air i always become air-sick
4 my cousin is at the university of reading she likes it very much
5 we saw some slides of west africa at the geography society they were very interesting

Each of the following examples consists of *three* sentences:

6 dr patel examined me carefully he could find nothing wrong he said i need not worry
7 we flew home by twa (trans world airlines) it was a very comfortable trip the hostesses were very helpful
8 i am visiting new york in the autumn it will be my first visit there i'm looking forward to it very much
9 everyone in england seems to think that all west indians come from jamaica there are many other islands i come from st lucia
10 sarah is a nice girl she is going to work for unesco she is a very good secretary

Each of the following examples consists of *four* sentences:

11 alan has just won a scholarship he's going to the usa he's already got a dip ed* he's going to get a ph d**
12 we lost our luggage at cairo airport it went on to pakistan we had no clothes at all we had to go and buy lots of new things
13 there was no clue to the murder no weapon a bare room just a very dead body (*See* section 16, page 9)
14 i have read chinese poetry only in translation i like the translations of arthur waley naturally i don't know how accurate they are i should like to be able to read the originals
15 my mother drinks lots of china tea when it's hot i don't like it myself i prefer coca-cola for this mother thinks i'm a savage

Each of the following examples consists of *one, two, three or four* sentences:

16 when i saw mrs smith she had just passed her driving test she was very pleased as you may imagine she asked me whether we'd go round to have dinner with her to celebrate tomorrow
17 in the end i stopped the argument by saying we could easily find the height of everest by going along to the library and looking up some reference books
18 if *a journey to the centre of the earth* isn't in the library, please get me another book by jules verne i think he's a wonderful author
19 at chinese new year all the children have lucky-money many firecrackers are let off there are many parties too
20 we saw a film about japan on tv last night there was some wonderful scenery but tokyo seemed rather crowded

* dip ed is short for Diploma in Education
** ph d is short for Doctor of Philosophy

Exercise 4

Put capitals, hyphens, and full stops as needed in the following passages. *Do not use any commas.*

1 *Six sentences*   my school is called st joseph's only boys go there i have been a pupil for two years my brothers go there too i like it very much i shall take my gce in three years' time

2 *Eleven Sentences*   the burglar opened the window he took out his torch the room was empty he jumped in suddenly a bell began to ring he put out his torch he made for the window again he stopped sgt williams and pc jones were standing at the window the burglar drew his gun it was a 33 calibre revolver

3 *Eleven Sentences*   we found the goat ill when we got home it was the prize-winning champion we had bought the previous day it was lying down on the straw its eyes were closed and it was hardly breathing we decided the goat must have escaped and eaten some poisonous plant i rang up the vet straight away he was out his wife answered the 'phone she promised to get in touch with him immediately he was in our district he would be with us shortly

4 *Thirteen Sentences*   the rain fell heavily the level of the river rose the water surged against the slender wooden supports of the only bridge for twenty miles it began to tremble we heard it creaking i decided to risk crossing it was vital to get to a hospital only at the hospital could i get help i switched on the headlights the landrover started into life i pointed the bonnet towards the bridge it lurched further every moment i put my foot gently on the accelerator

5 *Thirteen Sentences*   this examination was the most important for mary it was the final exam for her ba* she was very nervous as she sat down at her desk if she passed she might be able to go abroad to complete her studies to become a teacher she might even become a lecturer she looked at the paper her eyes could not focus she almost fainted she closed her eyes a moment and tried to concentrate then she saw that she could answer the questions easily there was one on the recent history and growth of the ussr and another on the usa she decided to write about russia first she took up her pen and began to write

*ba is short for Bachelor of Arts

Exercise 5

Put capitals, hyphens, and full stops as needed in the following passages. *Do not use any commas.*

1 many people love to gamble some of my friends say that gambling is wrong i do not believe it is if one does not spend too much money on it never expect to win think that the money is spent as soon as the bet is made winning should always come as a surprise

2 judge strong said that it was one of the worst cases he had ever had to try the evidence was shocking he could hardly believe it he said that smith would have to be sentenced to a long term of imprisonment to stop others from attempting similar crimes in future any other cases that came before him would be similarly treated

3 it was very quiet in the valley from where the car had crashed there came no sounds the shouts and screaming had stopped we clambered down the cliffs at the foot of them a swirling river barred our way we did not know how deep the water was the current seemed overwhelmingly strong the noise of the waters breaking on the boulders was so loud we could not hear any sounds that there might have been from the crash the battered boot of the car and the two back wheels could be seen rising above the bushes on the opposite side we looked helplessly at one another

4 the train stood a long time in the station the signals stayed at red the platform was swarming with refugees from all over the province and the police were trying to maintain order rumours were rife i desperately wanted a drink against the wall a tap was visible even in my distress i did not dare leave my seat once off that train i should never be able to get on it again i shouted to attract the attention of someone who might fetch me a cupful of water i thrust a tin cup out of the window and a handful of bank notes no one was interested in paper money now it could buy nothing a seat on the train or a handhold anywhere on the side was all that anyone wanted

5 near the pond where i had dropped mr wong's camera in the water was the monkey house i went in cautiously it was not my lucky day a large chimpanzee called zimba looked at me evilly i felt glad she was behind bars then she began to fumble with the catch of her door with one bound she was out she grabbed at my binoculars i held tight the leather strap broke the monkey swung up to an iron bar with surprising intelligence she took out the binoculars from their case i found myself being viewed by a monkey through a pair of zeiss binoculars worth fifty pounds the animal was looking through them the wrong way i

would look very small absurdly this humiliating thought angered me considerably then other people in the monkey house began to laugh this made things worse i did something very stupid

Question Marks

20 *Direct questions*

Use a question mark for a *direct* question (that is, where the actual words used are quoted), even if the question is made in statement form.

Examples: Have you seen my books?   Can you spare a minute?
You saw him?   You take sugar in your tea?

WARNING: A question mark is *not* used after a question reported in *indirect* speech (that is, where not all the actual words spoken are quoted).

Examples: He asked me whether I had seen his books.
I asked him whether he could spare a minute.
Compare these with the direct questions above.

WARNING: A question mark replaces a full stop. Do not write a full stop and a question mark together at the end of a sentence unless the full stop is indicating an abbreviation.

Example: Has your brother got his M.A.?

Exercise 6

Put question marks, full stops, capitals, and hyphens as needed in the following sentences.

1 i have an omega watch
2 we have some swiss money left, haven't we
3 did it rain here on tuesday
4 are john and barbara coming with us on our spring holiday
5 what time are the geography lectures
6 don't you think the new french mistress is very attractive
7 how often do you see captain lopez
8 where are mr and mrs wright going for the week end
9 i asked richard whether his uncle phillip was coming back from bombay for christmas
10 which model volkswagen is your teacher going to buy

11 the policeman wanted to know where m* brun's driving licence was, but his french was not adequate for the situation

12 the secretary was asked whether she liked her new remington typewriter, or whether she preferred her old hermes

13 please ask sally whether she knows where her aunt and uncle have gone

14 how will mother get to town now the bus is no longer running

15 do you know what the weather is like in the south of italy in autumn

* m is short for Monsieur

Exclamation Marks

21 Strong emotion

Exclamation marks show a strong emotion, such as surprise, anger, indignation, fear, joy, etc.

An exclamation mark may occur after one word, or a few words, or at the end of a sentence. If the exclamation mark is after only one or two words, you may start the next word with a capital or not.

Examples: Help! Throw me a rope!
Stop! we've left the light on!
Whatever you do, he's certain to win!
Hurray! I've got the job!

WARNING: Question marks and exclamation marks *replace* full stops. Do not use a full stop as well as an exclamation mark — unless the full stop is indicating an abbreviation.

Example: I've failed my B.Ed.!

Exercise 7

Put capitals, hyphens, full stops, question marks, and exclamation marks as needed in the following.

1 can you come on tuesday i should be glad if you can john and jenny are coming too do try to come i'll meet you at the corner of elm road

2 stay where you are can't you see it's a trap careful there's a wire running across the floor have you got a torch

3 my uncle arthur served for thirty two years as a non commissioned officer in the royal marines he retired last

november and has gone to live in devon it's a lovely part of the world anne and mother are going there for their holidays this summer

4   are you a do it yourself enthusiast my brother mark is he was given a book for christmas — 'the complete home handyman and decorator' now he is always at it the trouble is that his taste and my mother's are not the same you should have heard the row we had yesterday he said the french windows were old fashioned and draughty he wanted to take them out and brick up the wall at this mother said they were elegant and made the room cool in summer the worst thing was that he had started on the work when she came home he is only sixteen he is extraordinarily self confident or should i say self willed the funny thing is that it's mother who gave him the book she doesn't think it funny of course mark is too pre occupied with his new hobby to have any sense of humour either

5   Set out the following as five lines of verse.
there once was a lady of riga who went for a ride on a tiger they returned from the ride with the lady inside and a smile on the face of the tiger

3   Commas

22 *General comments on the use of commas*

The use of commas
Commas separate parts of a sentence.
They help us to understand the meaning of the sentence.

Reading the sentence aloud as a guide
Commas mark *some* of the pauses made in speech. If you read
your sentence aloud, where you pause, you *may* need a
comma.
But do not use a comma for every pause.
  Some pauses need other punctuation marks.
  Some pauses need no punctuation marks at all.
So reading your sentences aloud, and noting the pauses, can
only be a rough guide.

Firm rules and general guidance
There are a few firm rules on the use of the comma, but often
only general guidance can be given.
Whether to use a comma or not may depend on —
  the length of the whole sentence or parts of it;
  the emphasis you want to give to certain words;
  what other punctuation marks you are using in the
  sentence.
Two equally experienced punctuation 'experts' might well have
different opinions on some uses of the comma in a particular
sentence.

One general rule is worth remembering:
Commas should be used for a purpose

Unless a comma is needed to make the sense clearer, it is best
to miss it out.
It is quite possible to have quite a long sentence with few or no
commas in it. (*See* Exercise 3, no. 17)

Pairs of commas

Commas are often used in pairs.

If you need to use a pair, be very careful to write both commas down: a common mistake is to forget to write down the second comma.

23 Sometimes before 'and'

a) When 'and' joins single words or short word groups, do not use a comma before it, as a general rule.

Examples: I like physics and chemistry.
My sister and I will be going to the party.

But use a comma if necessary to make your meaning quite clear. Compare the following:
I am studying English literature and painting. (the painting is English painting)
I am studying English literature, and painting. (painting in general, not just English painting)

b) When 'and' joins two statements with the same subject, a comma is generally not needed, especially if the statements are short.

Example: I came home and turned on the radio.

But if the subject is repeated, or a new subject is introduced, a comma is generally used.

Examples: I took some food out of the refrigerator, and then **I** began to make supper. (repeated subject — bold type)
I opened the box, and **Michael** took out a cigar.
We stood waiting for a long time in the rain, and even so the **bus** went past without stopping. (new subject — bold type)

c) When several 'and's are used close together, use a comma to mark the *main* division.

Examples: We invited John and Mary, and Alice. (that is, John and Mary are married, or in some way 'together')
I read and write in the week, and at the weekends relax.
Richard bought a whisky and soda, and a gin and lime.

24 Sometimes before 'or/nor'

a) When 'or' or 'nor' joins *single words,* do not use a comma before it, as a general rule.

Examples: John or Jack will probably come with us.
A hot or cold meal would suit me equally well.
Ahmed neither smokes nor drinks.

But use a comma if necessary to make your meaning quite clear. Compare the following:
Would you like a cup of tea or coffee with rum in it? (the rum will be given with either)
Would you like a cup of tea, or coffee with rum in it? (the rum will be given only with the coffee)

b) When 'or' or 'nor' joins word groups, use a comma before it.

Examples: Everyone was covered with mud, or soaked to the skin.
Do as I say, or you will have to leave.
My cousin has no talent for drawing, nor have his children.

c) When several 'or's are used close together, use a comma to mark the *main* division.

Examples: I could not decide whether to go to the theatre or cinema, or stay at home.
Would you like cheese or ham sandwiches, or a full meal?

25 Usually before 'but'

a) Use a comma before 'but' in most cases.

Examples: The hotel was good, but expensive.
My sister worked very hard, but could not pass her examinations.

b) Do not use a comma before 'but' if other commas are needed close by in the sentence. This would break up the sentence too much.

Examples: Josette, tired but still hoping to win, continued to run.
Politely but firmly, I said that I wanted my money back.

c) When several 'but's are used close together, use a comma to mark the *main* division.

Example: The water was cold but refreshing, but no-one else would go in with me.

26 Always before 'for', 'as', and 'since' (when these mean 'because')

Examples: We stayed at the first hotel we could find, for we were tired out.
I left after an hour, as she had not arrived.
He did not go out, since he had no umbrella.

note: A comma is also used after clauses beginning with 'as' or 'since'.

Examples: As it was late, I took a taxi.
Since I had no cash, I gave him a cheque.

27 Special note: 'and', 'or/nor', 'but' appearing close together

When 'and', 'or/nor', 'but' appear close together, use a comma to mark the main divisions.

Examples: The job is interesting and varied, but not very well paid.
The new car is fast but safe, and very attractive to look at.
Please get me some brushes and paints, or some books.

Sometimes a comma is absolutely necessary to make the meaning plain, particularly if a choice is being offered.
Compare: Candidates should answer questions A or B, and C.
Candidates should answer questions A, or B and C.
Compare: On the tour you can visit Italy or Austria, and Switzerland.
You can visit Italy, or Austria and Switzerland.

Exercise 8

Put commas, capitals, and full stops as needed in the following sentences.

1 i can speak german and spanish equally fluently
2 we play both netball and hockey at our school
3 neither threats nor promises improved my brother's shocking behaviour
4 the paint was thick but usable
5 i must find a more interesting job or i shall go mad
6 marie could not work any longer in edinburgh as her work permit had expired
7 i went out to buy some books and came back with a typewriter
8 i opened the crate and found the cups broken

 9 the climate here is cold but not damp
10 i should become a doctor but i'm sick at the sight of blood
11 i'll bring the drink and you provide the food
12 my sister-in-law or her mother will look after penelope and muriel
13 you must take this chance to go abroad and study or you'll regret it all your life
14 stay here and have a drink and i'll ring for a taxi
15 mother has to work all day and cook and clean in the evenings and at weekends
16 hard work and determination are often more useful and more profitable qualities than occasional lazy brilliance and my brother's story seems to show this
17 i could not stay and listen to the end of the record for jim and joan were arriving at euston station and i didn't want to be late
18 my grandparents but not my parents like classical indian music and so i often go to their house to listen to it
19 my wife and i should like to visit france and spain but we have short holidays and little money these days
20 get some coffee and biscuits and i'll try and find mr cooper

28 Lists of words and word groups

a) Separate each item in a list with a comma: 'and', 'but' or 'or/nor' usually joins the last item of a list.
The final comma before this joining word is optional.

Examples: My new car is fast, roomy, and quite economical.
I should like a long, exciting, and unusual holiday this year.
We want a house near the shops, close to a bus route and not too expensive.
You could finish your homework, practise the piano and still come out.
We found the box, opened it, looked inside, but it was empty.

b) If no joining word before the last item is used, then a comma *must be used* to separate the last two items.

Examples: Insects were in the kitchen, on the balcony, under the bed.
The prisoner jumped out of the train, rolled down the embankment, disappeared into the woods.

c) Be careful to separate words and groups correctly. If you do not, you may give your sentence a meaning quite different from the one you intended.

Compare: I invited Mary, Elizabeth Jane, Anne, Michael Joseph, and Paul.

I invited Mary, Elizabeth, Jane, Anne, Michael, Joseph, and Paul.

Compare: To make this model you will need hardwood poles, brass, nails, steel hooks.

To make this model you will need hardwood, poles, brass nails, steel, hooks.

d) Place a comma between adjectives which can be written in reverse order.

Example: I live in a large, old house.

(a comma separates *large* and *old* because we could reverse the order here — that is, we could write: I live in an old, large house)

But: I live in a large brick house.

(no comma between *large* and *brick* because we cannot write: I live in a brick large house)

Exercise 9

Put commas, capitals, and full stops as needed in the following sentences. The use of commas is based on section 28.

1 rickshaws taxis open lorries and a surprising number of private cars crowded the roads
2 i love football tennis open-air swimming boating and in fact most outdoor sports
3 we found a flat piece of ground unloaded the car and began to put up the tent in the dark
4 the plane circled three times started to land and then climbed up again
5 people were lying on the floors of the wards in the corridors out on the verandahs wherever they could find a space to sleep
6 my new danish stainless steel cutlery has been ruined by that noisy and expensive dishwasher
7 my teacher saw the ruins of angkor-wat in indo-china the pyramids of egypt the acropolis in athens and i don't know how many other wonderful and famous places in a round-the-world trip he won in a newspaper competition
8 the bishop said in his sermon that men should do their work as well as they can not look for earthly rewards and help their fellows as much as possible
9 i found the key on the hotel desk took the lift to the fourth floor

got into my room and then remembered that i had said nothing
about the lost luggage

10 james is a good potter joan paints with considerable skill carol is
a singer but i seem to have no talent at all

Exercise 10

Put commas, capitals, and full stops as needed in the following
sentences. Use of commas is based on sections 23-28.

1 the zoo is well stocked with various animals birds and reptiles
but has no fish

2 in the high oak corner cupboard i could find only an old plastic
cup and a cracked chipped china plate

3 westerns detective stories old-fashioned comedies and such-
like rubbish are all we see on tv these days and daddy says he is
going to sell the set

4 my host told me that eating pancakes on shrove tuesday and
lighting bonfires on november 5th were well-known time-
honoured english customs and he was most surprised we did
not have them in our country

5 i don't greatly care for jazz pop swing or other kinds of modern
music but my children love it

6 the manager looked into my complaints and admitted there had
been a mistake but said it would take a week before i got my
money back

7 a dog and a cat and a goat and some white mice — i like
animals but this seemed rather a menagerie to live with and i
said i was sorry but i could not rent the house after all

8 i said i did not care much when he went where he went how he
went but he had to go at once or i would tell the police what he
had done

9 we have a charming swiss lady teacher for french and german
this week and perhaps for the whole term and we are all very
excited

10 i dislike waiting for buses but i had no choice yesterday evening
for i had left my purse at home and had little money with me

29 Words and phrases connecting sentences

Examples of connecting words and phrases:

however	further	besides
thus	therefore	nevertheless
nonetheless	finally	consequently
in addition	on the contrary	on the other hand
for example	worst of all	to crown it all
in the end	in short	

...... and many others

a) It is not always necessary to mark off such connecting words and phrases with commas. In fact single words and short phrases are not to be marked off unless one is aiming at a particular emphasis, contrast or dramatic effect.

Examples: We finally found the camera under a cushion. In the end we gave her the money.

But: Finally, we walked out.   . . . .*for emphasis*
On the other hand, you could be right.   . . . .*for contrast*
Worst of all, we had lost the map in the river.   . . . .*for dramatic effect*

b) Ambiguity and confusion:
Sometimes a comma must be used to make one's meaning quite plain.

Examples: Further exploration was impossible that winter.
Further, exploration was impossible that winter.

Both sentences are correct — but each has a different meaning.

Exercise 11

Put commas, capitals, and full stops in the following sentences. Use of commas is based on section 29. Mark off all connecting words and phrases.*

1 besides my father there were three other men in the boat
2 besides i like the chinese way of life too much to leave hong kong
3 you could on the other hand refuse to pay the fine
4 to make matters worse the man who took the money is a magistrate's son
5 consequently i'd be glad if you did not mention this to anyone
6 my best friend for instance has never ridden a bike
7 however i will come if you want me to
8 however much you ask me i shall stay at home
9 therefore please find enclosed a cheque for one hundred dollars
10 in other words you are refusing to help me

---

*As explained, connecting phrases need not always be marked off. However, mark them all off in these sentences, to show you clearly understand what connecting words and phrases are.

30 Adverbs and adverbial groups

Adverbs and adverbial groups tell us how, why, when, under what conditions, etc., something happened.

a) *Adverbs* An adverb is not normally marked off by a comma.

> *Examples:* I walked home **quickly**.
> He **carefully** opened the packet.

But adverbs may be marked off for emphasis.

> *Examples:* **Silently** and **swiftly**, David slid open the door.
> A voice shouted in the darkness, **threateningly**.

b) *Adverbial groups* The general guidance here is to mark off adverbial groups only if they are long, or if they need to be emphasized. Groups at the beginning of the sentence are more likely to be marked off.

> *Examples:* I left my clothes where I could easily find them again.
> While my father was out looking for a job, my mother cooked us a meal.

31 Participial phrases

The present participle is the part of the verb ending in *-ing*, such as **turning, finding, opening, seeing**.
The past participle is formed in various ways — it often ends in *-ed*: **turned, found, opened, seen**, etc.*
Phrases are often formed from these participles.
Participles and participial phrases are often marked off by commas.

> *Examples:* Before **going** out, he lit the fire.
> I sat against the rock, **facing** the mountains.
> **Defeated**, the team left the field.
> He fell back and bit his lip, **groaning**.
> I wandered around for hours, too **dazed** to think.

---

*the past participle is used with have/has to form the perfect tense: e.g.
I **have seen** a crash; he **has learnt** a new language; we **have finished**; etc.

Exercise 12

Put commas, capitals, full stops, and hyphens as needed in the following sentences.

1 we both went for a walk in central park
2 before the meeting i asked charles about the elections
3 unless we can get better seats i don't think i shall come to the play
4 when at last we arrived at the station in the centre of milan we found that the rome paris express had just left
5 if you would really like to come with us i'm sure there'll be room
6 under the shade of a large mango tree in the yard two men were sharpening cutlasses
7 interviewed by the police michael halliday refused to talk about the stolen goods found in his house
8 picking our way across the marsh with great care we reached the dry land safely and in quite good time
9 trapped by the ice our ship was helpless and in a dangerous position
10 washed up by the tide a bottle lay on the yellow sand

32 Adjectival clauses

An adjectival clause contains a verb and tells us more about the noun. It may be introduced by a word such as **which, who, whom, whose, that, when, where,** or the connecting word may be omitted.

The rule on adjectival clauses is firm, as there are two kinds of adjectival clause, one needing commas, and the other not.

Type 1 — Defining clauses (do not use commas)

The words in a defining clause *identify* the noun in the main clause. In the examples below the words in bold type tell us:

which mother rushed to hospital
which pen was lost
which girl won the prize

Examples: The mother **whose child was hurt** rushed to the hospital. (NO COMMAS)

The pen **(which) I lost** was a birthday present. (NO COMMAS)

The Mayor congratulated the girl **who won the prize.** (NO COMMA)

Type 2 — Non-defining clauses (you must use commas)

In this type of clause, the words do *not identify* a person or object. They give additional information about it. In the following examples, we know *which* mother (my mother), *which* pen (my new pen), *which* Paris (there is only one) is being referred to. The clauses in bold type give additional information.

Here the commas act like brackets (*See* chapter 8, page 42).

Examples: My mother, **who is 65**, is having a party next Saturday. (COMMAS)

Paris, **which is so attractive in spring**, is too hot in summer. (COMMAS)

I have lost my new pen, **which was a present from my aunt**. (COMMA)

Note that the meaning of a sentence may be altered by the use of commas.

Both these sentences are correctly punctuated.
a) The schoolchildren who have their meals at school are well fed.
b) The schoolchildren, who have their meals at school, are well fed.
But they have different meanings:
a) means that *some* children eat at school — and these are well fed;
b) means that *all* the children eat at school, and are well fed.

Therefore you should be always careful to make sure you have punctuated your sentences so as to get across the meaning you intend.

Exercise 13

Underline the adjectival clauses in the following sentences, and mark off the non-defining ones with commas. Also use commas, capitals, full stops, and question marks as needed.

1 mr heath who has been headmaster for twenty years is retiring in the summer to live in cyprus
2 this saturday i start painting my house which has not been done for several years now
3 unfortunately the man who came to lecture us last week forgot half of his slides on his visit to the canary islands
4 the day when i go abroad will be my twentieth birthday

5 we found the place where we had left our clothes now covered with water

6 i've had no trouble at all with that old car i bought last year from the motorway garage

7 my grandfather who was born in india still speaks bengali and my mother who was a little girl when he came back still has some doll's furniture he gave her it is beautifully made

8 we were seized by the greatest fear we had ever known but our leader who seemed to know no fear at all kept cheerful he was very brave

9 last sunday when i met you at church i forgot to ask you to come to see the play that we are putting on at school next month you can come i should like you to

10 are the hens we bought at the market laying any better now

33 Words in apposition

In the following examples, the words between commas are said to be 'in apposition' to the words in bold type — they give more information about the words in bold. Mark off such groups with commas.

Examples: **My mother's favourite film**, 'The Sound of Music', is being shown again at our local cinema.
Wilson, the police superintendent, took charge of the case.
Alice, my younger sister, is now Head Girl.
I now know his **secret**, that he spent five years in jail.
Is this **your idea of a joke**, to leave me without knowing where you had gone?

34 Comments

Short 'asides' or comments are marked off by commas.

Examples: My brother, I can assure you, will not let you down.
His uncle, it is said, is a millionaire.
Our team will win this match, that is certain.

Exercise 14

Put commas, capitals, full stops, and question marks as needed in the following sentences.

1 our headmaster's decision to ban all dances seemed unreasonable

2 did you know that prince our pet dog has just been run over by a bus

3 mr morrison's illness the result of too many years in the tropics
   has made him return to england
4 i detest his attitude to do as little work as possible
5 is it true that the club rule that ladies should not be members
   has just been altered
6 the 100 metres race was won believe it or not by joseph lee
7 my belief for what it is worth is that you won't be allowed to go
8 i'm not going to play in the game that's for certain
9 the police you must agree have been most helpful
10 ruth is when all is said and done still only a child

35 Names of persons spoken to

Use commas to mark off the names of people spoken to — but
do not separate the names of two people addressed together.

Examples: Joan, can you come here?
Can you hold this piece of work for me, John?
Jonathan and Josephine, you are making too much noise!
I do think, James, that you could work harder if you tried to.

36 Interjections and 'tags'

Interjections are words and phrases like **well then, of course,**
which are sometimes used in conversation. 'Tags' are short
phrases such as **don't you, can he,** etc. which are added to
sentences to form questions. These as well as **yes** and **no** are
usually marked off by commas.

Examples: Yes, we do agree with what you say.
Well then, get on with your work.
You can come tomorrow, can't you?
He won't help at all, will he?

37 Numbers and dates

We sometimes put a comma after the thousand figure in
numerals.

Examples: 1,567   234,589   2,356,965

But in mathematical working the modern (SI) style is to leave
spaces between groups of three digits.

Example: 12 754 129

A comma may be used in dates, but is optional.

Examples: 5th June, 1978   or   5th June 1978

Do not use a comma in a date if another comma is close by.

Example: He went to Japan on Saturday, 5th June 1978.

38 Inverted order

Sometimes the natural order of a sentence is reversed. In this case, use a comma, as in the examples below.

Examples: Ruth could not remember where she had left her camera.
But Where she had left her camera, Ruth could not remember.

I could not understand what the stranger was trying to say.
But What the stranger was trying to say, I could not understand.

WARNING — COMMAS: COMMON MISTAKES
1) *never* use a comma after a verb of saying or thinking in *indirect* speech:

Wrong: My father said, that I could not go out.
Right: My father said that I could not go out.
Wrong: I believe, that everyone should have the chance of a good school.
Right: I believe that everyone should have the chance of a good school.

2) *never* start a line with a comma

3) *never* write a full stop before a comma (like this .,) unless the full stop is to mark an abbreviation

Exercise 15

Put commas, capitals, full stops, question marks, and exclamation marks as needed in the following sentences. Use of the comma is based on sections 35-38.

1　mrs kennedy can you spare me a moment please
2　my passport is no 34678 and was issued on the 30th june 1970
3　how you can stand up for so long john i don't know
4　when jim arrives in london i really cant say
5　you can swim mary can't you
6　ladies and gentlemen the winning ticket number is 2343456
7　thank you miss wright i do take sugar

8 you could have phoned from the station couldn't you hazel
9 desmond have you invited hilda
10 thomas and louise stop playing in the mud please

Exercise 16

Put capitals, full stops, exclamation marks, question marks, and commas as needed in the following. All uses of the comma are included. Each example forms one sentence.

1 jonathan where are the books that i asked you to get from my desk
2 i asked barbara whether she had finished with *war and peace* yet and she said that she had
3 you would know whether the headmaster of central school mr charles wheeler is retiring at the end of this term or at the end of next term wouldn't you
4 unless i can win a scholarship i shall not be able to go abroad to study though i'd like to very much
5 the subject i did best in at st james' that was my school you know was art but i decided i could not make a living by drawing and so much against my wishes i had to go into barclays bank
6 as my aunt promised me a trip to the cinema as a reward i agreed to paint her door but i could not find either paint or brushes in the place where they were usually kept
7 why your cousin grumbles so much i really don't know for she has a good job and lots of spare time
8 did you know we've decided more or less definitely now that we're going to see harry's cousin in toronto next summer
9 we crept along the gravel path by the nurses' home as quietly as possible so that matron who had not given us permission to go out would not know of our return but unfortunately we had barely reached the open window when i sneezed and the lights were switched on
10 however we got home from visiting ronald and may to find the floor of our lounge littered with jane's papers thomas's maps and reference books his colour slides the negatives and unmounted transparencies of his trip to the andes my own notes and essays and all kinds of personal items; but nothing at all at any rate so far as we could see seemed to have been stolen which was puzzling indeed

Exercise 17

Put capitals, full stops, exclamation marks, question marks, and commas as needed in the following. All uses of the comma are included. Each example consists of more than one sentence.

1 my wife who does a lot of sewing has just bought a new electric sewing machine it has many gadgets it can do zig-zag stitches and embroider intricate patterns she does not want her old machine though it works very well would your wife like it she's very welcome to it do have it

2 the man who was interviewing me asked whether i knew what family of animals badgers belonged to i did not really know but in the end and after much help from him i managed to get the right answer what puzzles me is why i was accepted by the university i made such a fool of myself

3 if this plane is on time and we can get another at rome we should be in london in six hours do you think the hotel where we stayed last time will have any rooms james who was there last month said it was half empty but it may be more difficult at christmas if we can't get in there where else do you think we should try james asked me whether i had ever tried the queen's i haven't have you oh dear what was that noise is the plane going to crash

4 as we came out of the hall where the musical festival had been held we were met by john james and harry who all wanted to know whether we had had any luck we told them we had won first and second prizes they congratulated us and asked us to have a drink with them but we had to refuse as we had to catch the bus back home

5 at the table in the *golden cockrel* where we usually sat were two visitors evidently american we took another table near the door picked up the menu chose our favourite dish lobster and gave our order to the waiter mario who is the proprietor knows us well he came over to apologize he said he knew how much we enjoyed looking out over the mediterranean but as it was thursday he had not expected us on thursday it is true we usually go to the mainland assuring him that it did not matter in the least we were sipping our first glass of wine and glancing curiously at the backs of the visitors when one of them turned round to summon a waiter our eyes met there was immediate recognition and a flicker of fear

4 Apostrophes

39 Letters missed out

Use an apostrophe to show that a letter or letters have been missed out of a word. This is common in:

a) short forms such as **can't** for 'cannot'
   she'll for 'she will'
b) **o'clock** for 'of the clock' in time expressions
c) dates (**'69** for 1969 — or 1869, or 1769, etc. — the context indicating which century)
d) transcribing dialect speech

> *Examples:* It's late. I'm afraid I'll have to go now.
> We'll see you at 8 o'clock.
> I knew him in '52 in Pakistan.
> You can't think they'll do all the work for nothing.
> 'e took 'is 'at an' put it on 'is 'ead — indicating a dialect where *h* is not sounded — for 'he took his hat and put it on his head'.

WARNING: Do not confuse
it's = it is (It's time to go now.)
its = of it (The dog wants its supper.)
there's = there is (There's a party tonight.)
theirs = of them, belonging to them (Theirs is a fine house.)

40 Possession

Use an apostrophe to indicate possession by a person, an animal or an abstract noun (as in a time expression, for example)

a) Nouns having a plural in *s* or *es* (most nouns).
   Add: to the singular *'s*
        to the plural an apostrophe only

> *Examples:* The shopkeeper's letter appeared in the newspaper. (one shopkeeper writes)
> The shopkeepers' letter appeared in the newspaper. (several write)

b) Nouns having a special plural form (e.g. man/men; mouse/mice)
Add *'s* to both singular and plural.

Examples: The woman's conversation soon bored me. (one woman is talking)
The women's conversation soon bored me. (several women are talking)

c) Nouns having a singular ending in *s*
Either add *'s* (as noted in (a) above)
or an apostrophe only (to avoid writing the double *s*)
— this is more common.

Examples: Dickens's novels are still very popular.
One of Jesus' disciples betrayed him.

d) In some time expressions

Example: After an hour's delay, our plane took off.
I shall be back in three years' time.
Without a moment's hesitation, he dived into the sea.

e) After the last word of a noun group

Example: The captain of the school's speech was loudly applauded.

f) With schools and churches named after saints (add an apostrophe only if the name ends in an *s*)

Examples: St Peter's is the largest school in the city.
Our nearest church is St Barnabas'.

g) Names of shops and people's homes

Examples:
I am going to   the butcher's, the baker's,
                the Joneses', the Smiths',
                my aunt's, my grandparents',
                my aunt and uncle's,
                Smith and Brown's.
(Note that only the last noun of a group takes the apostrophe.)

WARNING: Never use the apostrophe with possessive pronouns:

his	ours
hers	yours
its	theirs

41 Some plurals

Normally the apostrophe is *not* used in forming plurals. There are, however, certain special cases in which it is helpful.

's indicates the plural of:

a) figures and symbols

Examples: I can't read the 7's very well — some of them look like 1's.

b) letters

Example: If you don't cross your t's, your handwriting will be hard to read.

c) words considered as items of language, not used as part of a sentence

Example: There are too many *and*'s in this sentence — rewrite it!

Exercise 18

Put apostrophes as needed in the following sentences.

1 Wed have brought ours if youd told us you couldnt bring yours.
2 My father and mothers wedding anniversary party starts at seven o clock.
3 I met him in 65 in Singapore. Yes, thats certainly Arthurs picture in the paper.
4 Anns losing her ring in the sand meant that we couldnt get to Paul and Marys before lunch.
5 St Marks first teams training hard for its first match of the season.
6 In three hours time were due to land at Londons newest airport.
7 Some of the horses shoes were loose, and its a wonder none of them went lame.
8 Theres a bakers in the village, and theirs is excellent bread.
9 The ladies cloakroom is on the right, just opposite the mens.
10 (DIALECT — some initial *h*'s missed out)
   She oisted erself up and eld er and out for er ot soup.
11 The two Δs are identical. I can easily prove that. Its easy.
12 Have I put too many es in that word? Its hard to spell.

5 Dashes

42 Lists

Use a dash before or after a list *if a collective word is used.*

Examples: We bought some new **crockery** — cups, plates, saucers, dishes.
I need some new **clothes** — a couple of shirts, a pair of trousers, and shoes.
Cameras, binoculars, jewellery, perfume — all sorts of expensive **goods** were hidden in the smuggler's car.

But: We bought some cups, saucers, plates, dishes.
I need a couple of shirts, a pair of trousers, and shoes.
Cameras, binoculars, jewellery, perfume were hidden in the smuggler's car.
(There are no collective words in these three sentences.)

43 Explanations and comments

A dash may introduce an explanation or a comment.

Pairs of Dashes: explanations or comments in the middle of a sentence will need a pair of dashes.

Examples: Susan had left all the lights on — another example of her carelessness.
My uncle Joe — he was himself an excellent swimmer — gave a cup for swimming to the school.

44 Dashes with other punctuation marks

A question mark or exclamation mark may be written before the second dash of a pair.

Examples: Mario — is that his name? — brought the coffee.

On Friday the 13th — a very unlucky date! — we moved into our new house.

45 Dramatic pauses

A dash may be used for a dramatic effect — to introduce something surprising.

Example: Roger Toynbee was sitting upright in his leather chair — dead.

46 Breaks in speech

A dash can indicate a pause or a break in speech.

Examples: 'Then — then I saw a — it was horrible. I just can't tell you how it — how it was — it was — you see, still alive! And when I — 'Jim suddenly stopped talking and looked hard at the door. The door was opening slowly.

Exercise 19

Put dashes as needed in the following sentences.

1 I at once packed some clothes a spare suit, a couple of shirts, some underclothes, and my bathing trunks just in case the weather improved.
2 I asked my sister Josephine she considered herself an expert on the cinema if the film at the Rex was worth seeing.
3 Charles said this is typical of him I'm afraid that he himself would provide everything chairs, tables, cooking utensils, and even an elephant if I needed one.
4 Old letters, circulars, bills, sheaves of notes, masses of paper all these littered the office floor where they had been blown by the wind.
5 It was it was I can't it was a horrible, slimy thing with a massive tail.
6 We looked with interest at what we'd found in Arthur's pockets a knife, some change, a wallet stuffed with notes and old letters, and most surprising this a key to Florence's flat.
7 My grandfather this is his peculiarity since the time he had been in Jamaica did physical exercises from five until five-thirty each morning.
8 Pottery his life-long hobby he now decided to make his career.
9 Our new carpet did you get that one you were thinking about? has not worn very well.
10 At the party on Tuesday what a party it was! James drank far too much, and Geoffrey who normally never drinks suddenly collapsed.

6 Colons

47 Lists

A colon may be used before a list *if a collective word is first given.*

Example: My sister finds all school **subjects** easy: French, history, maths, everything.
(A dash could also be used here — *See* section 42)

WARNING: The colon is never used if the collective word comes after the list. In that case, use a dash (*See* section 42).

48 Explanations and comments

A colon may introduce a comment or explanation at the end of a sentence.

Example: My name was not on the pass-list: I was not surprised.

WARNING: Do not use a colon to mark off a comment or explanation in the middle of a sentence.
Use commas (*See* section 34), dashes (*See* section 43), or brackets (*See* section 51). *See also* section 54.

Exercise 20

Put colons as needed in the following sentences.

1 We visited many famous cities during our tour of Europe Paris, Rome, Florence, and Madrid.
2 The car stopped after only six miles there was a leak in the petrol tank.
3 We had a nice surprise when we reached home Edna had cooked supper.

4 On my desk I found a pile of complaints the roof was still leaking, the water supply had failed, and the electricity was uncertain.

5 Inspector Barker took from his pocket certain articles a brooch, a penknife, and an ebony cigarette holder.

7 Semi-colons

49 Replacing full stops — joining statements

You may use semi-colons to join more closely two or more related statements which are really complete sentences in themselves.

Examples: The restaurant was empty; it was still early.
We entered the temple quietly; lights blazed in every corner; the festival had begun.

50 Replacing commas — marking main divisions

Use semi-colons to mark off the *main divisions* in a long sentence where there are many commas.

Example: The hunting knife, which had been sharpened to a fine edge, was lying on the table, glinting in the candle-light, sinister, threatening; the sleeper's right hand rested, or rather restlessly played, only inches from the jewel-encrusted hilt; every few minutes, the gigantic body shook hideously, as if somehow warned of our presence — and what we intended.

Exercise 21

Put punctuation marks as needed in the following. Each example forms one sentence.

1 the safe which had been broken into stood against one side of the room against the other a second safe seemed intact but mr browns assistant miss murray who looked very drawn and anxious was busy checking its contents

2 although we had been given very inadequate directions we found alberts house in a narrow street off st james square maria rang the doorbell maurice watched the back and i sat in the car with the engine purring under the shining bonnet

3 the clothes which had been left near the rocks consisted of a blood stained and tattered old shirt a pair of grey torn greasy overalls trousers which i thought i recognized as being the counts and finally half buried in the sand two sandals which did not make a pair one being perhaps size 8 and the other at least a 12

4 the way to the house lay through a clearing there seemed no one about we cautiously crept forward barely were we in the middle when a cry stopped us in our tracks

Exercise 22

Put punctuation marks as needed in the following passage. There are places where sentences may be separated by full stops or joined by colons or semi-colons. Punctuate as you think best, but use some colons and semi-colons.

we were told to take a taxi from st pancras station our train would arrive there at six o clock the address we were to go to was written on a piece of paper it was made up of words and letters cut from a newspaper i suppose this was so we could not recognize the handwriting even a handwriting expert could make nothing of that and we didnt suppose thered be any fingerprints on the paper the kidnappers would not make that sort of mistake the instructions were precise when we arrived at the house we were not to ring the bell nor even approach it but were to make for a telephone box at the corner of the street we should be in the box for 6 20 and expect to receive a call from max the leader of the gang if we informed the police then sandra would die we had no choice i rang up the station and asked john to come with me we agreed to get the 2 pm express for london

8 Brackets

51 Explanations and comments within sentences

Brackets — also called *parentheses* — mark off from the rest of a sentence information giving an explanation or comment.

The writing in brackets is independent of the rest of the sentence.

The writing in brackets may be removed, and a complete sentence remains.

Examples: Shakespeare (1564-1616) and Donne (1573-1630) were near contemporaries.

York (population 108,600) is about three times the size of Canterbury (population 32,790).

The lake ('Lake of Death' the villagers call it) lay to the south.

My brother (the wretch!) took all the chocolates.

52 Brackets used with other punctuation marks within sentences

a) Punctuation marks *inside* brackets. The writing in the brackets is independent of the rest of the sentence. Therefore it is punctuated separately. All punctuation marks may be used — except the full stop unless it is used for an abbreviation.

Do not start the writing in brackets with a capital, unless the capital is for a proper noun.

b) Punctuation marks *outside* brackets. Never use any punctuation mark before the opening bracket; any punctuation mark may be used after the closing bracket.

c) **note:** Question marks need special care.

Ask yourself whether the writing inside the brackets is a question or whether the whole sentence is a question.

Compare: We saw a very fine Sung vase (are you interested in Chinese Pottery?) at the museum.

Can you write me a short article (it need not be very long)?

53 Whole sentences as explanations and comments

Sometimes whole sentences are put into brackets. Sometimes more than one sentence is bracketed. In this case, a capital letter must be used for the first word, and the full stop written before the closing bracket.

Example: My copy of *Great Expectations* cost 75p. (You can get a paperback at 50p, but the print is not very good. It is not really good value.) Have you seen any other Dickens novels in cheap editions?

WARNING — BRACKETS
1) Brackets must always be used in pairs. Be sure you have used both brackets.
2) Never write an *opening* bracket (at the end of a line.
   Never write a *closing* bracket) at the beginning of a line.

54 Special note: commas, dashes, brackets, for comments and explanations

Commas, dashes and brackets may all be used to mark off comments and explanations. Sometimes you may use any of them, but the following guide can help.

a) Brackets must be used to mark off figures and translations of words.
   Examples: Our highest score (10 goals to nil) came in our last match.
   See-yau (soy sauce) was placed on each table in the Chinese restaurant.

b) Brackets must be used to mark off a complete sentence or sentences. *See* section 53.

c) Choose commas for short asides and comments.
   Example: My father, I am quite sure, would be glad to come.

d) Choose dashes for longer comments and explanations.

   The dash is the strongest marker. See section 43.

Exercise 23

Put brackets, dashes, or commas as you think best in the following.

1 The puppies there were seven of them were getting bigger.
2 All the family were looking forward very much to our holidays it was the first time we had been away for four years.
3 I have just been reading George Eliot have you read *Middlemarch?*
4 My mother was annoyed when we were late for lunch how she hates unpunctuality but she became more cheerful in the afternoon.
5 Denmark area 16,608 sq. miles has a population of 4,767,597 Automobile Continental Handbook, 1970.
6 Can you come to see us on Thursday I can take you home later in the car?
7 Is your Siamese cat a 'queen' that is the word, isn't it?
8 My teacher's harshness 'What a little fool you are!' he always seemed to be saying did not help me to understand mathematics.
9 I cannot afford any more private lessons in English I'm getting married soon, and I am saving all I can; thank you for all the help you have given me.
10 We saw five houses I know that was too many for one afternoon — a large detached house, a bungalow, a converted cottage, a farmhouse, and a small terraced house.

9 Quotation Marks*, Italics, Underlining

55 *Words actually spoken — quotation marks only*

Quotation marks are used to separate words *actually spoken* by someone, from the rest of a sentence.

Both the sentences in the examples below could be written without the quotation marks — but the use of quotation marks emphasizes that the words were spoken by John, in the first example, and the daughter, in the second — *and that the writer himself does not necessarily agree with them.*

Examples: John told me he would 'never work for such a fool again'.

My daughter says her flat is 'unfit for a dog to live in'.

WARNING: Be very careful to quote *only* the words *actually* spoken. Indirect statements and questions are not marked off by quotation marks.

Compare: 'You are late,' he told me. (Direct statement)
He told me I was late. (Indirect statement)
'Why have you come?' she asked. (Direct question)
She asked why I had come. (Indirect question)

You may use single ('......') or double ("......") quotation marks for any of the reasons given in this chapter, but be careful to:
  end with single, if you *start* with single
  end with double, if you *start* with double

Remember: quotation marks are always used in pairs. Make sure you have written both opening and closing quotation marks.

---

*Quotation marks are also called 'inverted commas'.

56 Marking off words in a special way

Quotation marks, underlining (in handwriting and typing), or italics (in print) may be used for any of the reasons given in the next 5 sections (57-61). They indicate that there is something special about the words marked off in this way.

Examples: I read it in the <u>Daily Express</u>.

I read it in the <u>Daily Express</u>.
I read it in the 'Daily Express'.

57 Titles of books, newspapers, magazines, plays, films, etc.

Remember that if the title of a book etc. is the same as the name of a character in it, quotation marks, italics, or underlining may be essential to avoid confusion. Compare the third and fourth examples below.

Examples: I read 'The Economist' every week.
Have you see the film version of *Oliver Twist?*

I find *Jane Eyre* fascinating. (the book is fascinating)
I find Jane Eyre fascinating. (the character is fascinating)

58 Names of ships, houses, hotels

Names of ships, houses, hotels, etc. are often marked off — but this is not absolutely necessary.
Do *not* mark off the names of churches, schools, and public buildings.

Examples: The *Star of India* sails on Tuesday.
The 'International' is the best hotel in town.
'The Pines' was certainly an imposing house.

But: St Paul's Church and the Houses of Parliament attract many visitors each year.
The Sacred Heart Convent School is opposite Government House.

59 Foreign words

If a non-English word is used, it is generally marked off.

Examples: We all had *boeuf à la mode.*

I was quite bored with the lecture on *hubris* in Greek tragedy.

60 Words referred to as items of language

If a word is referred to as an item of language — not being part of the structure of the sentence, then it is marked off.

Examples: Look up 'synopsis' in the dictionary, please!

'Semi-automatic' means that you have some control of the machine.

61 Words not chosen by the writer

In the following three examples, you can see that the writer does not believe that 'peace', 'traitors', and 'progress' are the right words to use. But they are words that have been used by other people — the writer in fact is criticizing the use of the words.

Examples: 'Peace' for the Romans often meant death and slavery for their victims.

The 'traitors' were taken out into the yard, and immediately shot.

'Progress' in the twentieth century means more noise, more smoke, and great expense for everyone.

62 Proverbs and quotations

Example: 'To err is human, to forgive, divine,' as Pope says.

63 Emphasis

Use only underlining, or italics in print — but *not* quotation marks — for emphasis.

Examples: My cousin is *very* handsome.

We came home *drenched.*

Exercise 24

Use quotation marks or underlining as necessary in the following sentences.

1 Fagin is a disreputable character in Oliver Twist by Charles Dickens.
2 Necessary is often spelt incorrectly.
3 What does all-inclusive mean in your price-list?
4 Have you seen Far from the Madding Crowd at the Odeon?
5 My brother swore he would not apologize to that scoundrel whatever happens. *(make it clear that some of the brother's words are being quoted)*
6 You ought to be able to distinguish there from their by now!
7 I don't call the engine smooth and silent whatever the advertising says.
8 Where does the quotation no man is an island come from?
9 I could not understand what the waiter meant by vitello. I think it is an Italian word, isn't it?
10 I explained that the doves are the more peaceable and the hawks the more warlike members of the government.

10 Direct Speech — conversation reported as it is spoken

64 Basic patterns — one speaker, one or a few sentences

Quotation marks Single or double quotation marks enclose *all words actually spoken.*

Capital letters Write a capital when direct speech starts — even if this is within a sentence — *see* examples 6,7,8,11 on page 50.
Do *not* write a capital when direct speech starts again in a sentence — *see* example 3.

Question marks and exclamation marks These replace full stops and commas.
Never write a full stop or comma *plus* an exclamation mark or question mark.

More than one sentence Close quotation marks after the whole speech. Do *not* close them after each sentence.

Full stop or comma? *Study example 4.* A full stop is used, not a comma, because if the words *he said* are removed, *two* sentences are left — *see* example 2.
Now study example 3. A comma is used because if *he said* is removed, *one* sentence is left — *see* example 1.

Colon A colon is sometimes used instead of a comma to introduce direct speech, as in examples 7 and 8 (commas could be used here instead).
The colon is often used after an introductory collective term — such as 'these words'.
The colon may also emphasize that direct speech follows.

Plays The form in example 11 is used in plays only. The words in brackets show how the words are spoken. They are a guide for the actor.

Relative position of marks Study the examples below very carefully to see how commas, full stops, question marks, and exclamation marks are placed in relation to the quotation marks.

If a whole sentence of direct speech ends with quotation marks these must come after the full stop, question mark or exclamation mark as in the following examples.

Examples: 1 'We shall come back at 7 o'clock, when your husband is at home.'

2 'We shall come back at 7 o'clock. Your husband will be at home.'

3 'We shall come back at 7 o'clock,' he said, 'when your husband will be at home.'

4 'We shall come back at 7 o'clock,' he said. 'Your husband will be at home.'

5 'We shall come back at 7 o'clock, when your husband will be at home,' he said.

6 He said, 'We shall come back at 7 o'clock, when your husband will be at home.'

7 He spoke very insistently: 'We shall come back at 7 o'clock, when your husband is at home.'

8 He spoke to her in these words: 'We shall come back at 7 o'clock, when your husband is at home.'

9 'When will your husband be at home?' he asked. 'We want to see him.'

10 'We must see your husband!' the visitor insisted.

11 **Visitor** (insistently): We shall be back at 7 o'clock. Your husband will be at home.

Words or phrases quoted

If the quotation is less than a complete sentence the closing quotation marks precede the final punctuation mark.

Examples: 1 He summed up the performance tersely as 'abysmal'.

2 The performance, he complained sharply, had been 'little short of a fiasco'.

3 He described the performance as a 'humiliating, total flop'.

Exercise 25

Punctuate these sentences according to the patterns 1 to 5 on page 50. In each case there is only one speaker.

1 its too late to go to the odeon now
2 well im not coming im staying at home
3 the newspapers are late on sundays frank replied
4 i have not read that book said john you must get it for me from the library
5 it was twelve oclock when the party finished he told me we had to get a taxi home
6 evening classes for drawing are all booked up the secretary told us
7 i now have a new camera michael said with a light-meter on it
8 but we have just seen inspector drew was the unexpected reply
9 if you are going put in anne youd better stop arguing and go if youre not going just stop arguing i want to read
10 the lighthouse restaurant is famous for its fish he said ill take you all tonight

Exercise 26

Punctuate the following according to the patterns 1-11 on page 50. In each case there is only one speaker.

1 im afraid i shall have to take statements from you all superintendent morris said as he took out his book
2 soldier roughly get up do you hear get up   (as in a play)
3 if that is all youre going to say uncle i protested i may as well leave you
4 can you help me mend my car i asked its a renault youre good at mending cars arent you
5 dont mention it exclaimed our host i was glad to be of help is there anything else i can do now
6 we could take a ferry direct to spain explained mr alexander its more comfortable but its more expensive than crossing the channel and motoring down through france
7 i replied nobody would think of doing a thing like that you must be mad whatever gave you the idea
8 my wife who was born in holland has never been back there explained captain arthur thats why were visiting amsterdam this summer

9 this is said miss grey lifting up the vase my most valuable possession
10 this is what he said to me you have deceived me you have lied to me why did you do it

65 Quotation marks within quotation marks

If you have to place one quotation within another quotation, change from single to double quotation marks, or the other way round, as you place the quotations.

Remember that underlining (*italic* in printed matter) may be used instead of quotation marks for titles of books, etc. This often looks neater. Compare 7 and 8 below.
Be careful to place commas and full stops correctly in relation to quotation marks. *Study examples 1, 7 and 8.*
Be careful to place question marks and exclamation marks correctly. *Study examples 2,3,4,5 and 6.*
Do not write two question marks or exclamation marks together, though they might seem to be necessary. *Study example 5.* Keep the first mark only.

Pairs of quotation marks Quotation marks must be used in pairs. Be sure you have written *both* quotation marks of each pair — and that single quotation mark is paired with single quotation mark and double with double.

Examples: 1 'I think the greatest of Shakespeare's plays is "King Lear".'
2 'She definitely said "I will never do that!" ' my brother insisted.
3 'Have you read "Faster Reading"?'
4 'I have just read "Can you Read Faster?" '
5 'Have you read "Can You Read Faster?" '
6 'Is there a French proverb like "Look before you leap"?' I asked.
7 'The librarian definitely said, "I've got your brother's copy of 'Hard Times' ",' my sister told me.
8 'The librarian definitely said, "I've got your brother's copy of *Hard Times*",' my sister told me.

Exercise 27

Punctuate the following passages of direct speech. In each case there is only one speaker.

1 did you enquired mrs ellis see the longest day at the ritz last wednesday

2 my father said you cannot be a soldier michael told me those were my fathers very words

3 i said are you quite sure that you haven't got my copy of improve your swimming

4 my sister janet was sitting reading her copy of schoolgirl in the corner theres a good article in here she said looking up its called are you good enough to be an air hostess do you think i am

5 when you say mischief-makers i burst out angrily you simply mean people who disagree with you why are you so dishonest

66 One speaker — two or more paragraphs

At the beginning of every paragraph — write quotation marks.
At the end of every paragraph except the last — do *not* write quotation marks.
At the end of the last paragraph — write quotation marks.

Example:

' _____ ' he said. '_____. _____

_____. _____. *(no quotation mark here)*

'_____. _____. _____

_____. _____. *(no quotation mark here)*

'_____.'

67 Change of speaker

Each time there is a change of speaker you should:
a) write quotation marks at the end of the first speaker's words;
b) start a new paragraph — indent the writing;
c) write quotation marks at the start of the next speaker's words.

Example:

'_____,' said Jonathan.

'_____,' replied Mary. '_____

_____.   _____.'

'_____,' added Elizabeth. '_____

_____.'

Ann broke in excitedly: '_____!   _____

_____?'

'_____,' answered Elizabeth.

Exercise 28

Punctuate the following passages of direct speech. In each case more than one person is talking.

1 do you often spend your holidays here at the hotel ofira no this is the first time replied my companion on the hotel terrace which commanded such a fine view of the aegean sea do you he looked at me enquiringly not finishing the question no i dont come abroad often this is my first visit to these parts then perhaps we can explore the neighbourhood together was the eager reply i have a car i suggested what about going up the coast to the monastery in the morning

2 have you seen my new york herald tribune no well you might help me to look for it instead of just sitting there and saying no i might but i wont why not because if once i find it you will .do nothing but read it all morning and i want to go shopping

3 do you know a poem called ozymandias i asked my father yes i had to learn it by heart at school its by shelley isnt it i really dont know i had to confess its a clue in a crossword do you remember how the first line goes i met a traveller from an antique land my father began thats it i broke in thanks i can do it now

68 Special uses of dashes, hyphens, and series of full stops in direct speech

This section reminds you of information given earlier in sections 14,19 and 46.

a) Use a dash to show a sudden break in speech (*See also* section 46).

Example: 'I told you that he —' I began.
'I'm sorry, but I don't want to hear any more about it,' my brother broke in.

b) Use a series of full stops to show a gentle break — either caused by weakness, or used for some special effect (*See also* section 19).

Examples: 'And if I don't do what you want me to . . .' his voice was mocking. I knew I could in fact do nothing. I was powerless.

'Please try to . . .' the voice faded to a whisper as the dying man sank back into unconsciousness.

c) Use hyphens to suggest stuttering or stammering (a speech defect) (*See also* section 14).

Example: 'C-c-can you t-t-tell me the t-t-time?' she stuttered.

11 Punctuating Letters

Sample Letter

14 Newby Street,
Ireton,
Nottingham N14 3SQ.

Telephone: Nottingham 234578

6th May, 1978

The Manager,
The Crescent Restaurant,
High Street,
Sheringham S13 2LB.
Norfolk.

Dear Sir,
     I visited your restaurant for lunch last Monday, and I think I may have left behind a pair of binoculars. Unfortunately there is no name in the case, but they are a pair of 8 x 30 Zeiss binoculars. If I have left them with you, perhaps you would be good enough to 'phone me at the above number, reversing the charges, as soon as convenient, as I do not want to trouble the police with reporting the loss if the binoculars are safe with you. I apologize for the trouble I am causing you.

Yours faithfully,

John Featherbrain

John Featherbrain

This is a formal letter — a letter on a business subject sent to someone the writer does not know personally.

A personal letter — a letter to someone you know personally — is set out in the same way, but you do not start the letter by writing the name and address of the person you are writing to; this is written on the envelope only.

Commas A comma may be written at the end of each line of an address — except the last line.
Write a comma after the greeting (*Dear Mary, Dear Sir,* etc.).
Write a comma after the polite close (*Yours faithfully, Yours sincerely,* etc.).

Full stop A full stop may be written after the last line of the address, but nowadays this is considered optional.

Capitals Write a capital for the main words in the greeting (*Dear Katharine, Dear Sir, Dear Aunt and Uncle,* etc.).
Write a capital for the *first word only* of the *polite close* (*Yours faithfully, Yours sincerely,* etc.).
Write no capital for other words in the polite close.

No punctuation mark Write no punctuation mark after the signature.
Write no punctuation mark after your name if this is typed under the signature.

Address on the envelope Set this out like the inside address — in the sample, the address of the restaurant to which John Featherbrain is writing.

Block and sloping layouts In the sample on page 56 the addresses are block: the left-hand edge is straight. In personal letters written in longhand, the writer's address and the address on the envelope are often sloped.

Block and indented paragraphs The paragraph in the sample letter is indented: the first line starts a short space in. In typed letters, every line may start at the same place, like the addresses in the sample, though the paragraphs will be separated by a space. That layout is called 'block'.

Exercise 29

Set out and punctuate correctly the following formal letters. Any punctuation mark may be needed.

1   571 stanley road kirkstone lancashire england 19th september 1978 the manager hotel del sol bilbao spain dear sir i should like to book rooms at your hotel for myself my wife and our two children aged 12 and 8 for the three nights the 3rd to the 5th august inclusive if you can offer us accommodation could you please quote terms yours faithfully s g jones

2   the red house lenton on sea norfolk 2nd september 1978 the sales manager manor garden furniture ltd heaton norris stockport cheshire dear sir i bought a garden swing seat from you by mail order in june and have had it in use in my garden since then the top member of the frame has partially come away from one of the uprights because of a faulty weld i think the fault is likely to put a great strain on the rest of the frame and is potentially dangerous i feel you will be willing to put this right under your guarantee but as the frame is so large i wonder whether you would prefer to have this returned to you or for me to have the repair done locally i have been quoted six pounds for the complete job including dismantling and reassembly yours faithfully s w kay

Exercise 30

Set out and punctuate the following personal letters. Any punctuation mark may be needed.

1   rose cottage yeldford devon 21st may 1978 dear aunt thank you so much for the watch its just what i wanted im so glad it has a luminous dial and a second hand i shall take great care of it father and mother bought me a new bike a raleigh you may remember the last one was stolen last year im having a party this afternoon and im expecting my guests any time now so i will write at more length later i do want to tell you about louises visit last week your loving nephew simon

2   ocean view hotel la toc castries st lucia west indies 11th january 1978 dear jane the weather here is wonderfully warm i wish you were here to share the sea and sun i met your friends the kings yesterday evening and they want to be remembered to you i am enclosing some photographs they took they have a camera which develops them instantly yours affectionately colin

12 Revision

Exercise 31

A punctuation quiz

The following questions test your knowledge of the guidelines to
punctuation set out in this book. You can check your answers very
easily. After each question you can see two numbers in brackets:
the first refers to the section, the second to the page where you
can find the answer. So the answer to question 1 is in section 2,
page 1.

*Try to do all these questions — answering them forms a complete
revision of all the main principles of punctuation in this book.*

1 Which is correct — english or English? Give your reason. (2/1)
2 Do names of the seasons start with a capital letter? (WARNING
 p. 4)
3 Are any commas needed in this sentence? If so, say where and
 why. (32/26)
   Joan of Arc who was burnt at the stake in 1431 was made a
   saint in 1920.
4 What three punctuation marks may be used to show that some
 kind of additional information or some kind of explanation is
 being given, in a sentence like this:
   Our visit   it was the first we had made to Poland   was
   a pleasant one. (54/43)
5 What punctuation mark would you use to give the impression
 of stammering? (14/8)
6 You might use either of two punctuation marks in a sentence
 like this — after a 'collective word' and before a list. What are
 the two punctuation marks?
   I like all sorts of fruit   apples, oranges, pears, bananas.
   (42/36   47/38)
7 Are any commas needed in this sentence? If so, say where, and
 give reasons.
   We left our bicycles near the old iron bridge. (28/22)
8 Which punctuation mark indicates a dramatic pause? (45/37)
9 If a long word is divided between two lines, it must be divided
 between syllables — and a hyphen must be used. Is the hyphen

written at the end of the line or at the beginning of the next line? (9/6)

10 'Whenever you pause in reading aloud, you must write a comma.' Is this true? (22/17)

11 Where must you *always* write a capital in direct speech? (64/49)

12 In writing the title of a book, some of the words should be given a capital letter. Which ones? (6/3)

13 The title of a book may be indicated as such in three ways. What are they? (56/46)

14 When is it particularly necessary to mark off a book title as such in some way to avoid misunderstanding? (57/46)

15 What is the difference between *its* and *it's*? (39/33)

16 Are capital letters used for days of the week? (2/1)

17 We never/sometimes/often begin a line with a comma. Which is true? (WARNING/p.30)

18 Are capital letters used for points of the compass? (WARNING/p.4)

19 When is a full stop written just before a comma? (WARNING/p.30)

20 How do we show that a word is a foreign word or a word used in an unusual or special sense? (58/46 59/47 60/47)

21 How do we mark off the name of a person we are speaking to? (35/29)

22 In dialogue, each change of speaker means a new set of . . . . - . . . ., and that a new . . . . must be started. Fill in the blanks. (66/53)

23 We never/sometimes/often end a line with an opening bracket. Which is true? (WARNING/p.43)

24 If direct speech continues into a second sentence in the same paragraph, *without a change of speaker,* which of the following should you do?
   (a) put no quotation marks at the end of the first sentence and no quotation marks at the start of the second;
   (b) put closing quotation marks at the end of the first sentence, but put opening quotation marks before the second;
   (c) put no quotation marks at the end of the first sentence but put quotation marks before the second. (64/49)

25 Give an example of an indirect question:
   (a) do you need a question mark at the end of it? (20/14)
   (b) do you use quotation marks — and if so where? (WARNING/p.14)

26 Which of the following is correct, at the end of a personal letter?
   (a) Yours sincerely   (d) Yours Sincerely,
   (b) yours Sincerely,   (e) Yours Sincerely
   (c) Yours sincerely,   (f) yours sincerely,
                                      (Chapter 11/56)

27 What punctuation mark indicates surprise or strong emotion? (21/15)

28 Are adverbs normally marked off by a comma? (30/25)

29 If direct speech is continued into a second paragraph without change of speaker, which of (a), (b), or (c) suggested in question 24 applies? (66/53)

30 When do we write **their's**? (WARNING/p. 35)

31 Which of the following is correct at the opening of a personal letter?

(a) Dear John,	(d) Dear John.
(b) dear John.	(e) dear John,
(c) Dear John	(f) dear John

(Chapter 11/56)

32 What punctuation mark must you place after the signature in a letter? (Chapter 11/56)

33 Two punctuation marks are always used in pairs. Which are they? (WARNING/p.43 65/52)

34 If a direct speech is marked off by single quotation marks, how would you mark off a quotation in this direct speech? (65/52)

35 What is a series of full stops like this .... used for? (19/10)

36 What must you write in a formal or business letter that you do not write in a personal letter? (Chapter 11/56)

37 If you have a complicated sentence with many commas in it, how might you mark the main divisions? (50/40)

38 What punctuation mark separates items in a list? (28/21)

39 Are dashes always used in pairs? (42/36 43/36 45/37 46/37)

40 Do you need a capital for **uncle** in the following sentence?
    I asked my uncle Peter to get me a model aeroplane. (5/2)

41 What is a colon used for? (47/38 48/38)

42 Are full stops the only punctuation marks that can come at the end of a sentence? (15/9 20/14 21/15)

43 Where are capitals used in poetry, and not in prose? (8/4)

44 Are capitals used for the names of any school subjects? (WARNING/p.4) If so say which ones.

45   This is your hat.
    This sentence is written in a statement form. It could be read aloud as a question. Would you then write the sentence with a question mark at the end, or not? (20/14)

46 Is an apostrophe ever used with **his** and **hers**?
    If so, explain when. (WARNING/p. 35)

47 How do you indicate that a group of words is a proverb? (62/47)

48   John (getting angry, and lifting up his stick): How dare you say that!
    When do we punctuate dialogue in this way? (64/49)

49 What is a semi-colon used for? (49/40 50/40)

50 Which of the following is correct?

    (a) My sister said that we were late.

    (b) My sister said, that we were late. (WARNING/p. 30)

Exercise 32
Comprehensive Revision Exercise

The following revise all punctuation rules given in this book.

1 *Set this out as a letter*

   58 riverside terrace buxton derbyshire 23rd august 1978

   dear shirley and colin we got back from spain only last night and found your letter waiting for us what a wonderful surprise were so glad youve got the job you want and deserve and our warmest congratulations and best wishes for your future in japan were very envious especially on this chill late august day of our so called summer sunny spain and the costa brava and its playas* sounds much more exotic than beach doesnt it it all seems so far away now were enclosing a small present for you we hope it is light enough for you to take how are you flying my brother harry went boac by vc 10 and said it was a wonderful flight were sorry youre leaving so soon i dont suppose youll have time to come over to see us and we cant come to see you paul is working at st marys hospital two days a week now if you can come over however please do theres a train that leaves st pancras at 1015 and gets to our place about one o clock i could come and pick you up in the old austin cambridge yes its still going just about do try and make it give our regards to uncle tom and auntie may yours sincerely jenny

2 *Punctuate for two speakers*

   ive just finished reading the spy who came in from the cold have you read it no but i saw the film did you see the film i dont go to the cinema much in fact ive not been for ages was it a good film good it was tremendous

3 overwork to keith said trevor means two hours reading a day hes a lazy brute hes trevor stopped abruptly as keith came in been working keith asked trevor pleasantly you look tired here sit down this is a nice chair

4 tiger tiger burning bright in the forest of the night the first two lines if no more of blakes poem the tiger are well known to everyone but how many people know of blakes other poetry in fact blake 1757 1827 is considered by many critics to be one of our major poets some would say greater than william

---

*playas is the Spanish for *beaches*. Punctuate to indicate that the word is not English.

wordsworth 1770 1850 who was born only a little later though he lived much longer

5   these were the three members of the expedition frank he was the leader a tall sunburnt and incredibly tough man with twenty years climbing experience behind him james who was very fortunately as things turned out a doctor but for him phillip would certainly have not survived and phillip very cheerful and resourceful he was responsible for the photographs and round his neck swung as a rule two or three cameras

6   *Punctuate for two speakers*
stuck in the mud and unable to move an inch i could do nothing but shout how long was it before help came it seemed hours i think in fact it was about an hour and a half were you frightened frightened i was petrified with fear the tide was on the turn if help had not come i should have been caught and drowned you must get some rest now did dr smith leave you any sleeping pills yes theyre over there can you get them theyre the red ones thanks

7   the shops having all closed for the night there were three things we could do try and borrow a bed from our neighbours let rose sleep on the floor or ask her to share a bed with my sister my sister would not like that and knowing how fitfully my sister sleeps i didnt suppose rose would either the neighbours were not very good friends but i decided to ask them mrs o grady came to the door

8   his words you should have no trouble in finding us became a bit of a joke when we first got lost in the winding and intersecting lanes first george would say it and i would laugh then i would say it and george would laugh but when the fuses on the car blew leaving us immobile and in darkness and there was no sign of the house the joke lost its attraction when the snow began to fall we felt even more humourless and when our host at last came along with a party to look for us in fact we were only a few hundred yards from the house and they had heard the car stop suddenly they found two cold and stony faced guests huddled in the front seats sorry i should have given you a map never mind well fix the car in the morning come along weve a fire inside

9   *Punctuate for two speakers*
whats your book the man from devils island came the reply it sounds an exciting title its an exciting book i dont know where you get the time for reading pat oh you have to make time i never read anything nowdays nothing at all i read in bed id just go to sleep

10 at his desk inspector charles reeves second in command of the criminal investigation department cid for short opened the file lit a cigarette and began to read the notes with attention across from him on the hard chair where hundreds perhaps thousands of suspects had been interrogated julian wondered how many had ever come out of police headquarters free men he tried hard to keep still and remain impassive he wondered what was in that file it looked very full and there were several photographs inside outside from across the park he could hear the heavy thudding of the pile drivers building the foundations for the new hotel his hotel the inspector looked up he was not smiling there was a critical pause julian clark no julian ford why did you change your name a foolish thing to do i think you have some explaining to do

INDEX